Jill Sykes
Beanie Kaman
Emily Elisa Halpern
Karrie Ross

FM Fine Art Gallery
Los Angeles, CA

September 2015.

I0469873

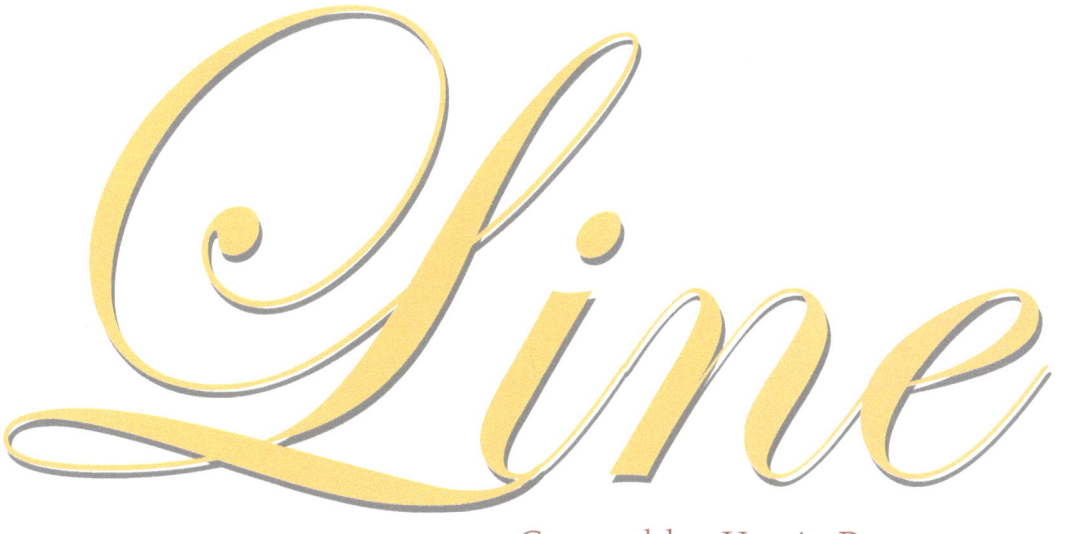

Line

Curated by Karrie Ross

L I N E

with Jill Sykes, Beanie Kaman, Emily Elisa Halpern, Karrie Ross
Curated by Karrie Ross

Karrie Ross: 12516 Washington Place, Los Angeles, CA 90066
Visit her website at www.KarrieRoss.com.

Printed in the United States of America

Book Design by Be It Now! Karrie Ross

L I N E

Artists are the creators and keepers of history. They work to bring the hidden to light. We can go on for ever and still take something for granted until an artist brings it to our attention... if only for a little while sharing their fascination.

I believe there is a story in everything and these exhibiting artists each share their own unique 'take' on line, and the exploration of... please meet

Jill Sykes "discovery"

Beanie Kaman "direction"

Emily Elisa Halpern "disconnect"

Karrie Ross "distortion"

Together "we are L I N E !"

I think line is taken for granted. When was the last time you really viewed the horizon, or thought about the act of standing with others to buy morning coffee. How about when you drive on the street, do you even think about it being divided into rows by lines for safety. Or when you pick up a pencil or pen and lines begin to appear in the form of words, an expression of self. Lines just are.

The artists in L I N E really push the limit here, and they might not have even realized that their art was exampling line... I didn't until I looked for it... line was in the shadows becoming form, in shapes watching it morph, scratched with emotions in dance, and trying to find a safe place in their awkward vibration.

"It" all starts with a line.

September 2015

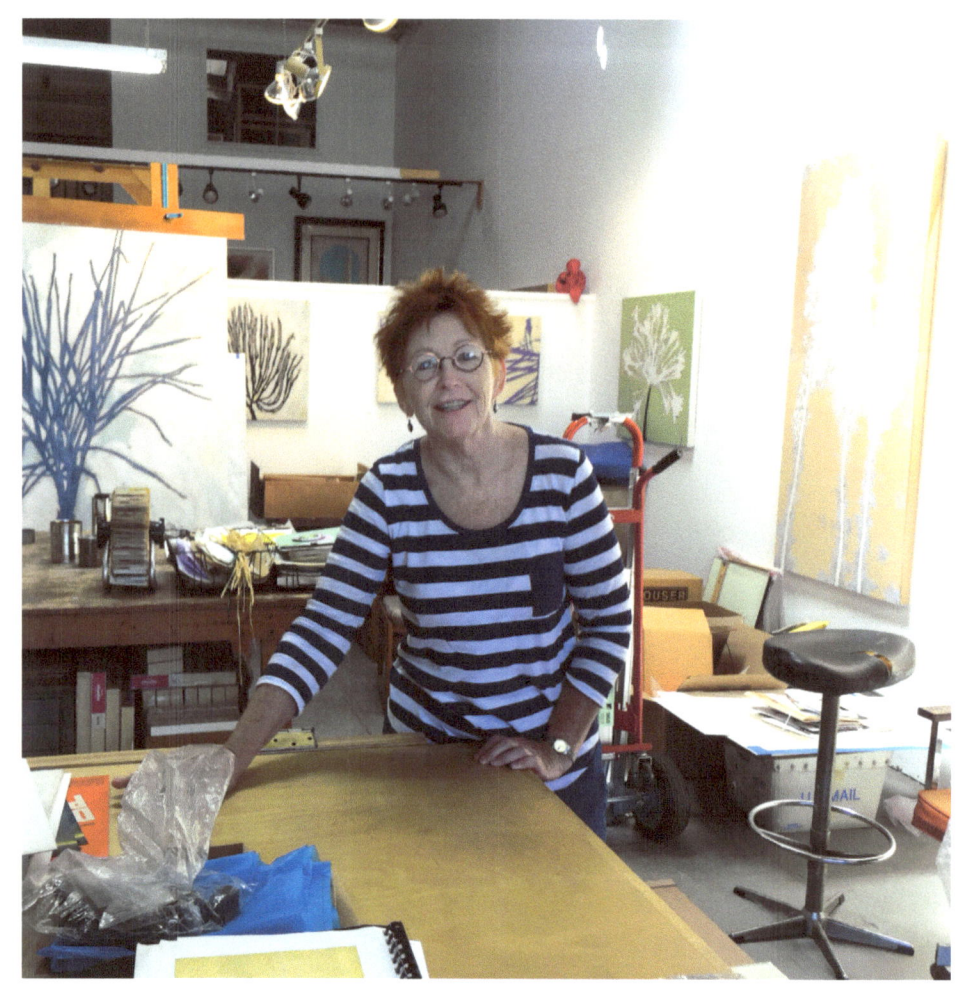

LINE

Jill Sykes

dis·cov·er·y

1. the action or process of discovering or being discovered.

Line is not always seen. It can be imagined, remembered, discovered. In discovery I learn about who I am and possibly even why. It's like finding a solution to a puzzle – eventually it seems to appear with a bit of prolonged looking, even when I'm not fully conscious that I am, in fact, looking.

As a child I drew incessantly – my mother could not keep enough paper in stock, so eventually she installed a small blackboard in the kitchen, and later lamented that those drawings could not be saved. I became fascinated with the shapes and forms of everyday objects and animals, Discovering that our family cat had bending joints in his legs and then making a drawing of that was somehow astonishing to my parents. All I did was pet the cat and there it was – a knee. Recording that little anatomical discovery on paper seemed the next logical step, even to 4 year old me.

So my eyes – and hands – do the discovery work for me. They seem to ever be searching out the new, the interesting and unusual juxtapositions in nature. It's a constant search, I know now, for that "safe place," that protective shelter that is welcoming and open. A shadow, a line, or an area of negative space between the two – this is exciting stuff. Like finding out cats have knees.

My work in L I N E   is all about that search and my ultimate fascination with shape and form and quiet. These images all evoke a kind of shared sanctuary – as if I were literally peering through the hanging branches out onto the world. There is always – always – something new to discover beyond the shadows.

www.jillsykes.com

September 2015

L I N E

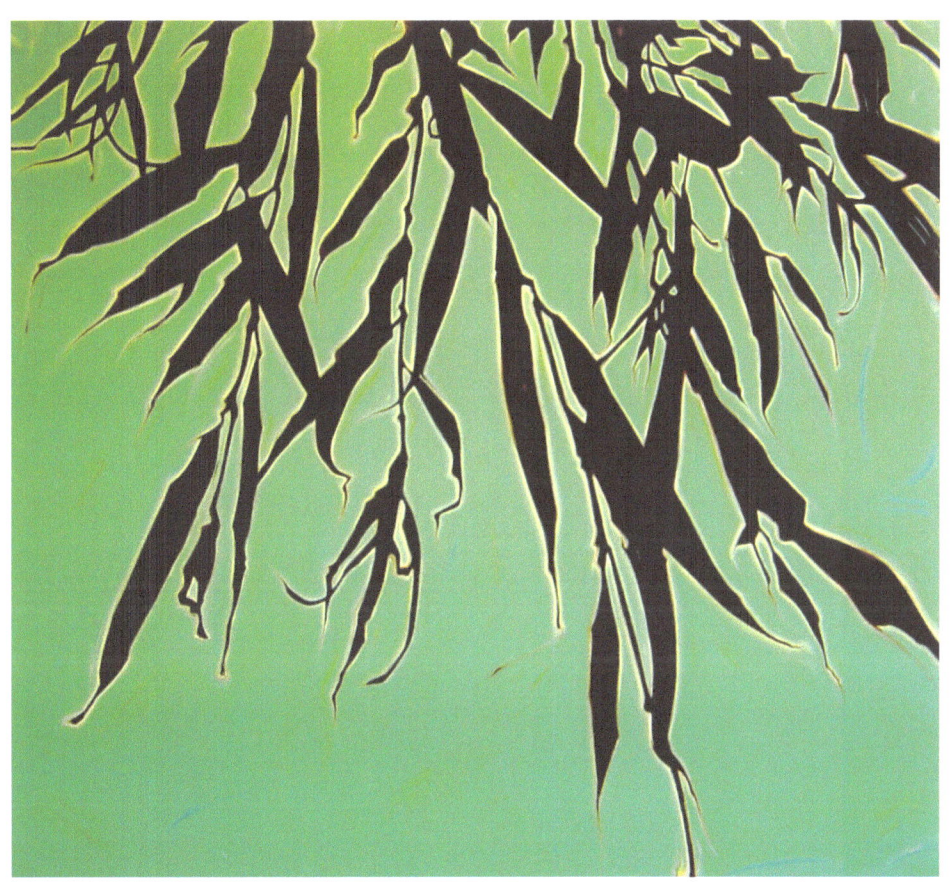

Lux Aeterna
48" x 54"
oil on canvas
2006

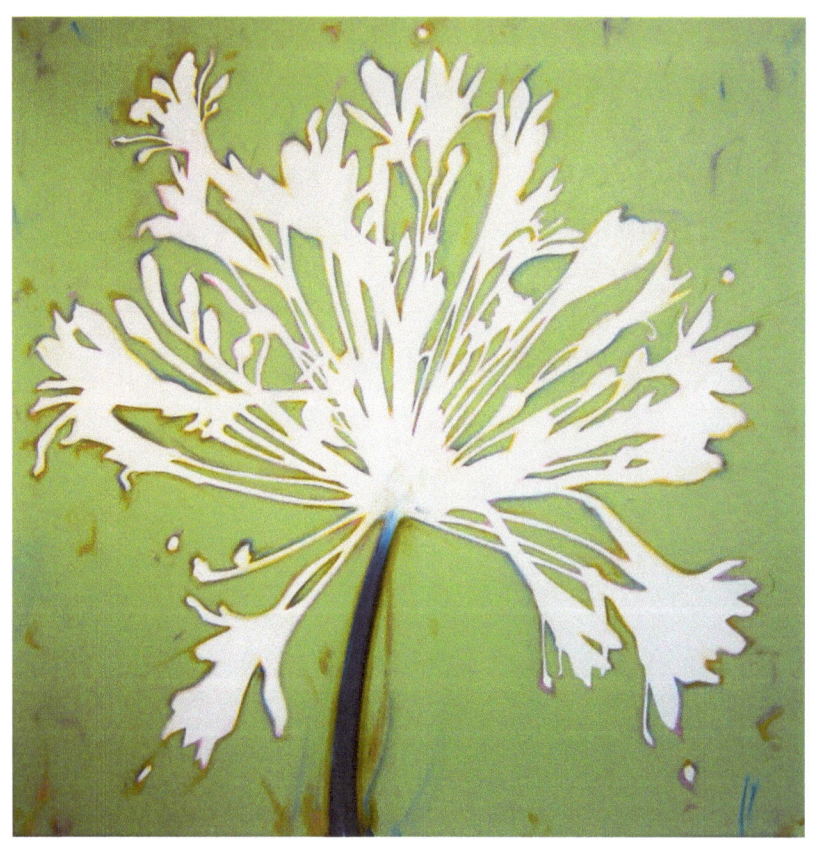

Ghost
30" x 30"
oil on canvas
2014

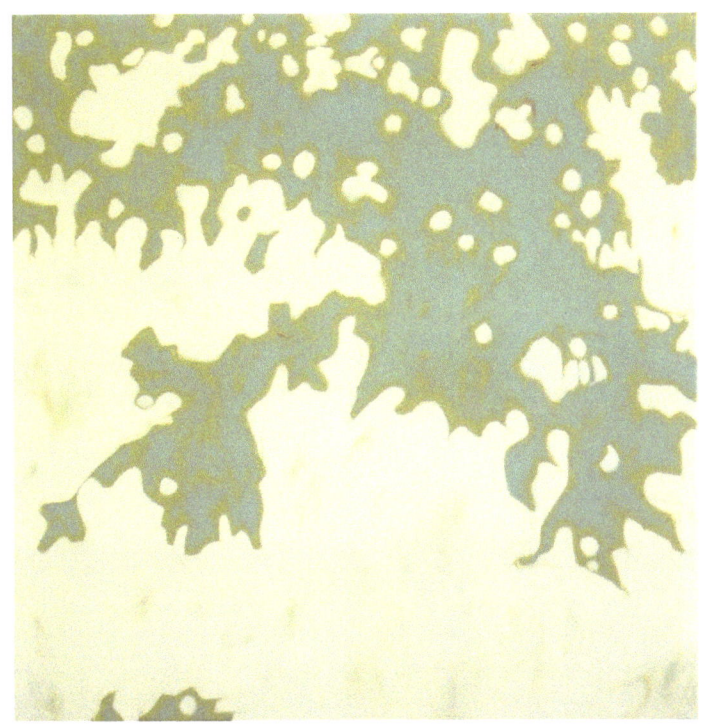

Skylark
24" x 24"
oil on canvas
2007

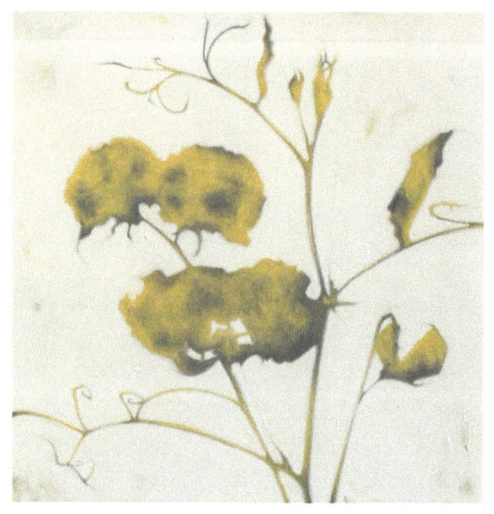
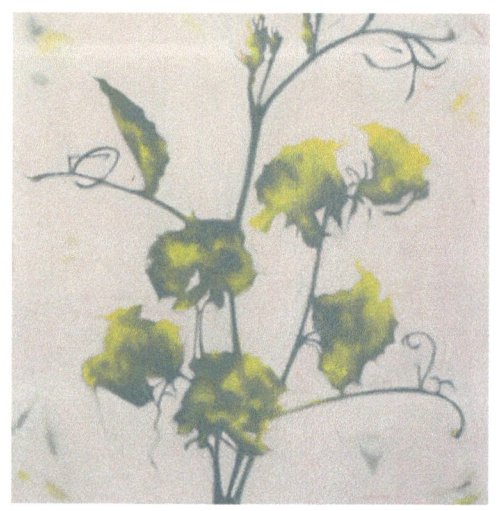
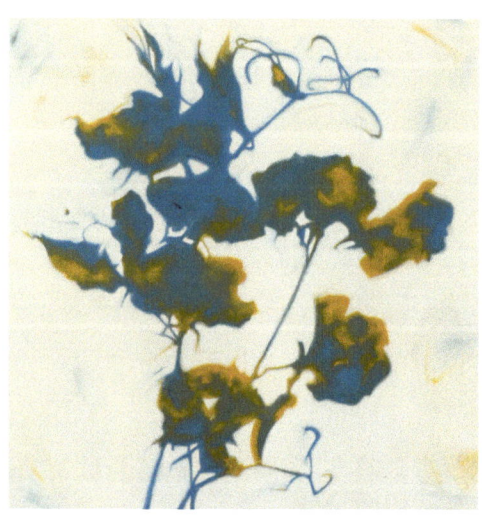
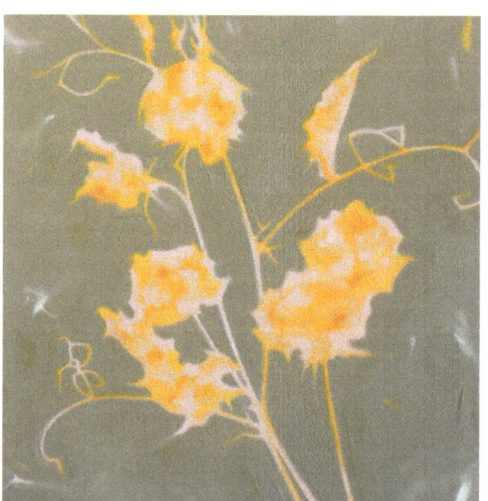

LINE

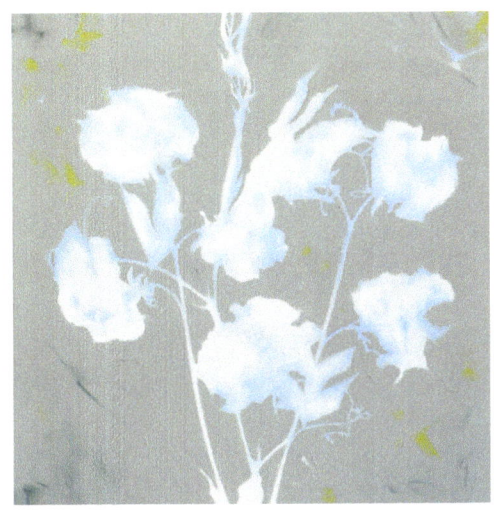

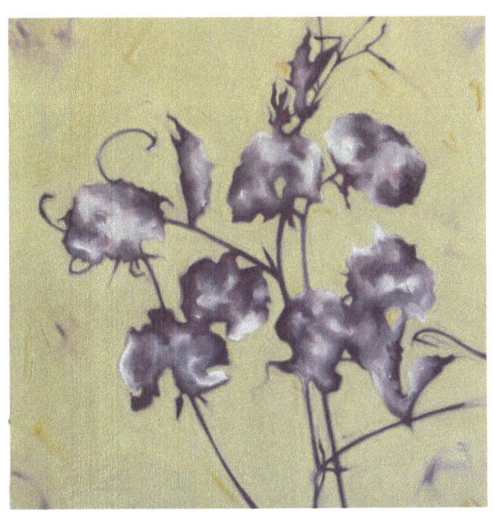

SweetPea Suite (set of 6)
14.5" x 14.5" each
oil on 6 panels
2013

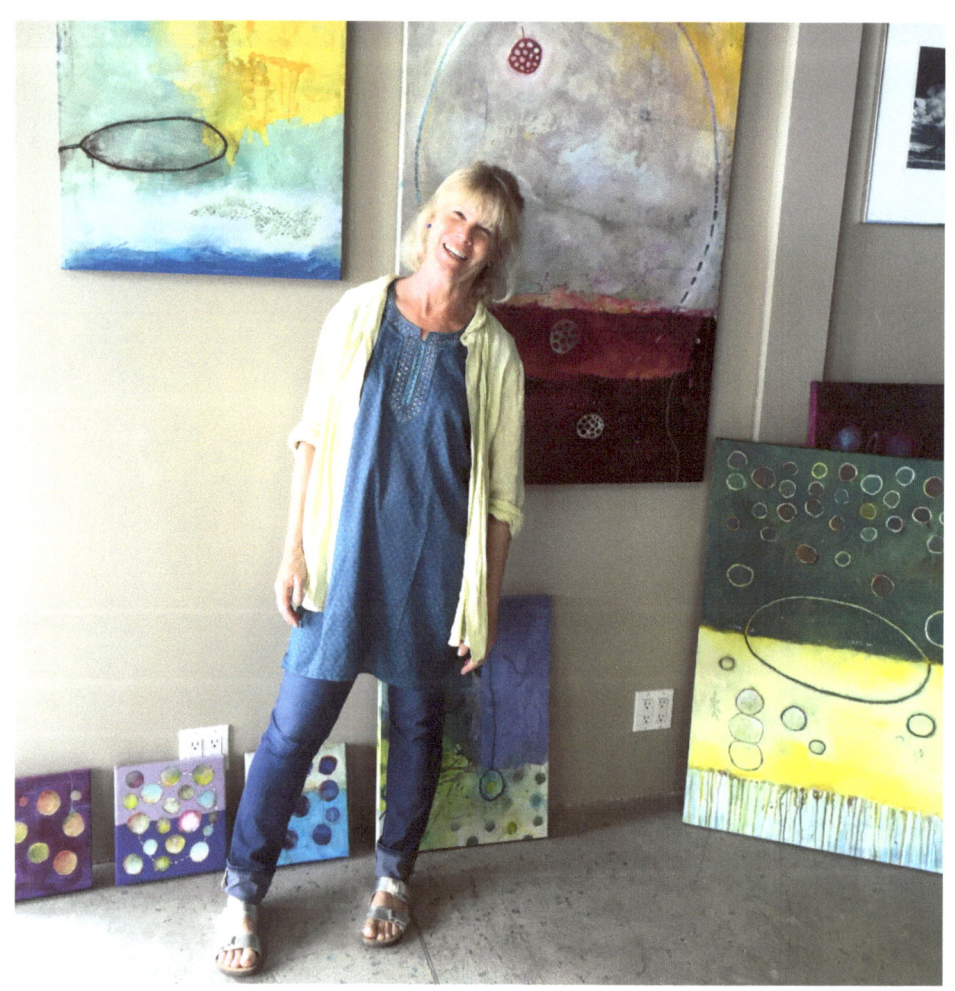

LINE

Beanie Kaman

di·rec·tion

1. a course along which someone or something moves.

When I am working, line forms a direction that becomes a path to follow. Often the beginning is too far away to see, nor is the end in sight. But following the path, in whatever direction it may lead, will always bring new discoveries and inventions.

I grew up on a farm in Connecticut, with acres of untouched forest surrounding the pastures. It was always exciting to open the gate into the woods and take off to be in that beauty of wildness and freedom. I loved wandering in, feeling small among the large pines or like a giant from Gulliver's Travels while examining the delicate beauty of the green green moss growing on a tree stump. There was no path to follow, I just made my own way and followed the direction that my sight took me to next. It was my own small piece of heaven.

My paintings do reflect that sense of direction, of wandering within the space, finding my way in and out, here and there. I delight in walking the line between painting and drawing, playing with dimension and flat space. I am happy to let the line either form a structure or simply lead the eye around the painting. It is always an ongoing adventure of self-discovery and visual storytelling, with the hope that the viewer might walk along with me, and include their own story as well.

www.beaniekaman.com

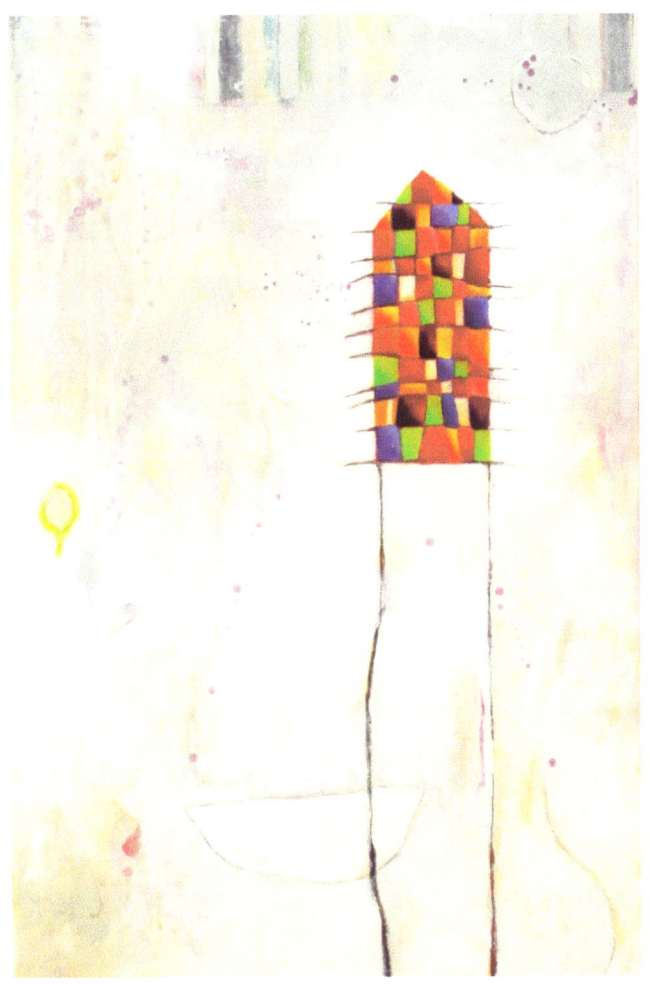

House With A View
50" x 34"
acrylic, dried pigment, pencil on canvas
2014

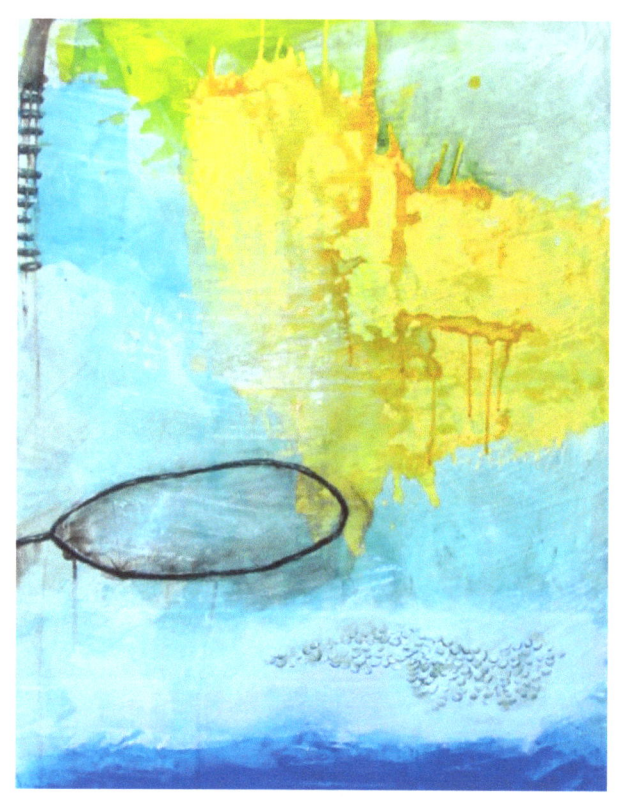

Magnify
30" x 24"
acrylic, dried pigment on canvas
2015

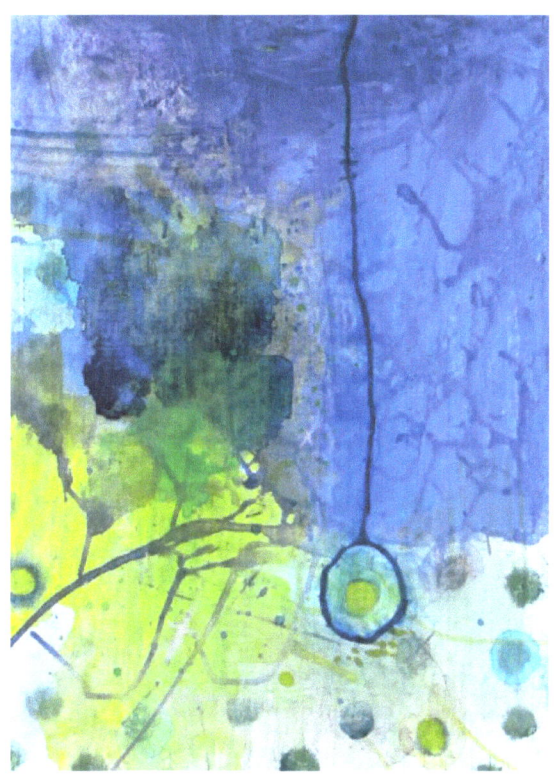

It Might As Well Be Spring
24" x 18"
acrylic, dried pigment on canvas
2015

Aqua Sea (top left)
10" x 10"
acrylic, dried pigment on canvas
2015

Directions (top right)
10" x10"
acrylic, dried pigment on canvas
2015

Rocky Planets (bottom left)
10" x 10"
acrylic, dried pigment on canvas
2015

Seed Pod (bottom right)
10" x 10"
acrylic, dried pigment on canvas
2015

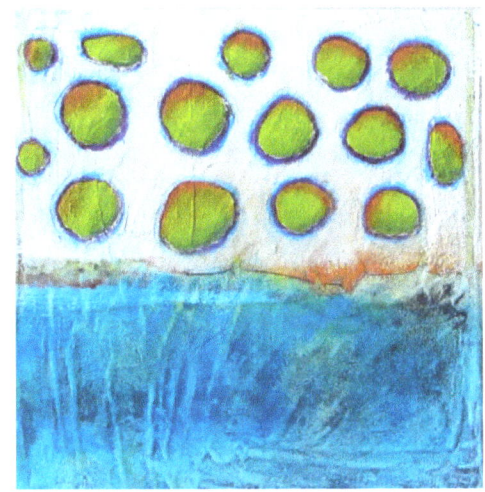

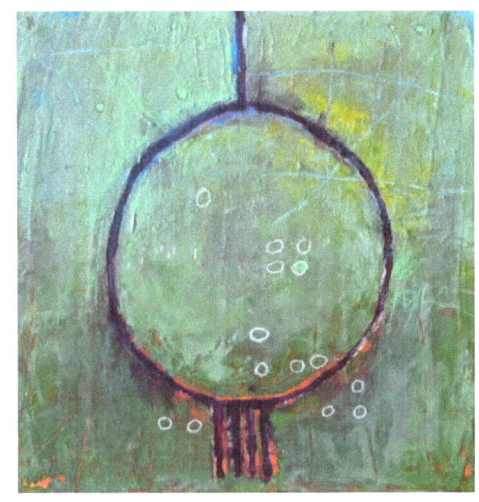

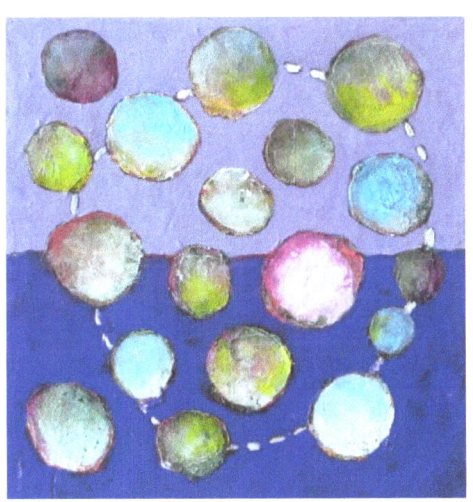

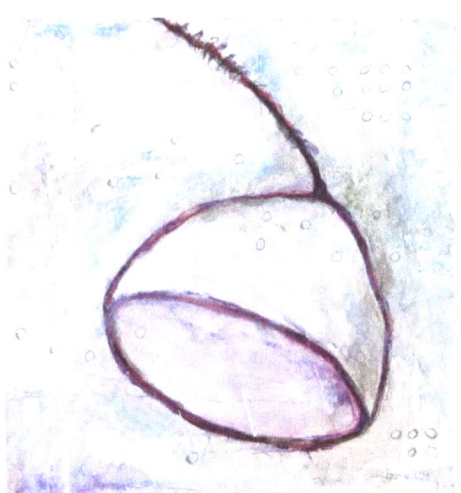

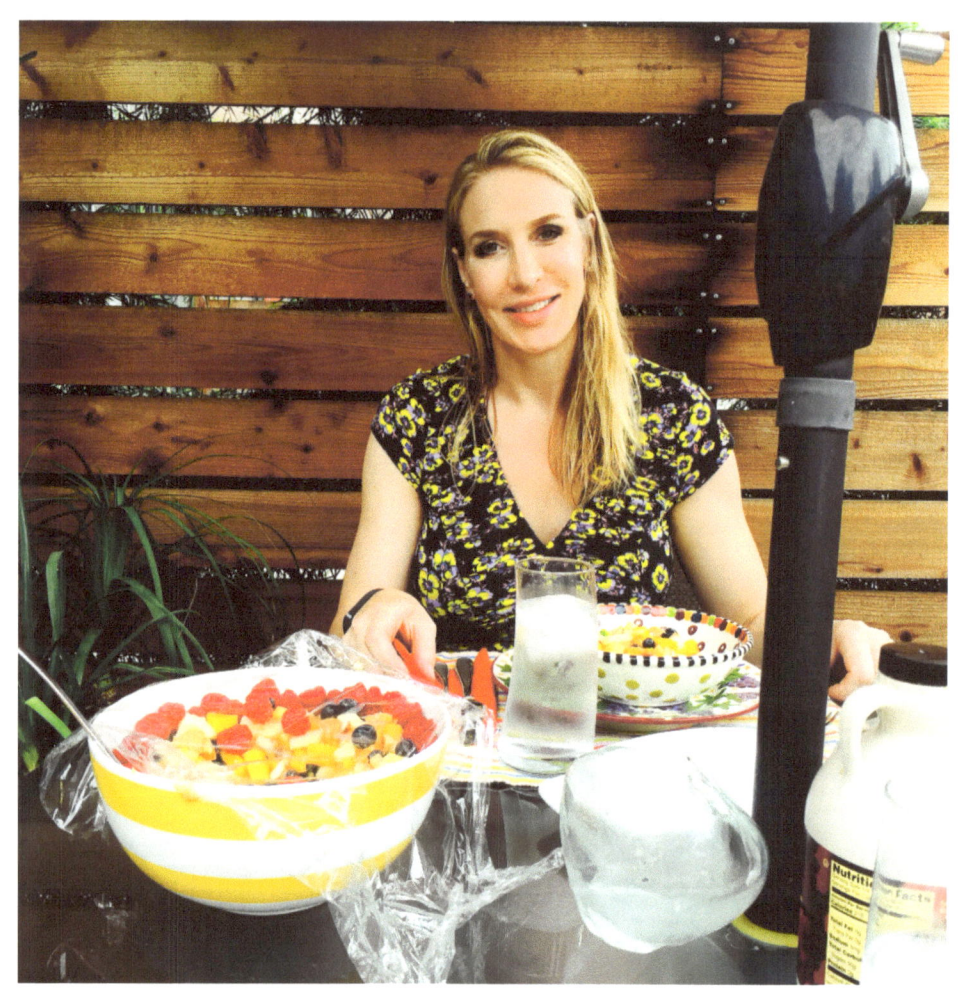

LINE

Emily Elisa Halpern
dis·con·nect

1. break the connection of or between.

Painting is a struggle. Every painting is a battlefield where an internal dialogue fights to come to fruition. Often, I destroy my work. In order for clarity to be found, my best work has come when I disconnect from inner voices and allow my subconscious to latch onto an idea.

When I was a child, my family had a summer cabin in the woods of Montana. I didn't have many art supplies, but always liked working with my hands and would create art work with things I found around me. I once created a portrait of my family out of deer poop. It was a really good likeness of everyone. Ever since then, I have found that when I allow my mind to disconnect and wander, I ultimately feel more connected to what I'm doing and have a clear vision to follow.

Lines allow us to connect and disconnect. A life line, a line of communication, an outreached arm, a ladder. A line can be a metaphor for how we are doing—fragmented or thick, strong or fragile. Lines take us on a journey and can bind us together or leave us unravelled. Lines appear in my work in the form of flying and floating contraptions, rocks and snakes, acrobatic high-wires or form ambiguous circles. The imaginary spaces are disconnected from reality, an exploration of my inner life.

www.emilyehalpern.com

LINE

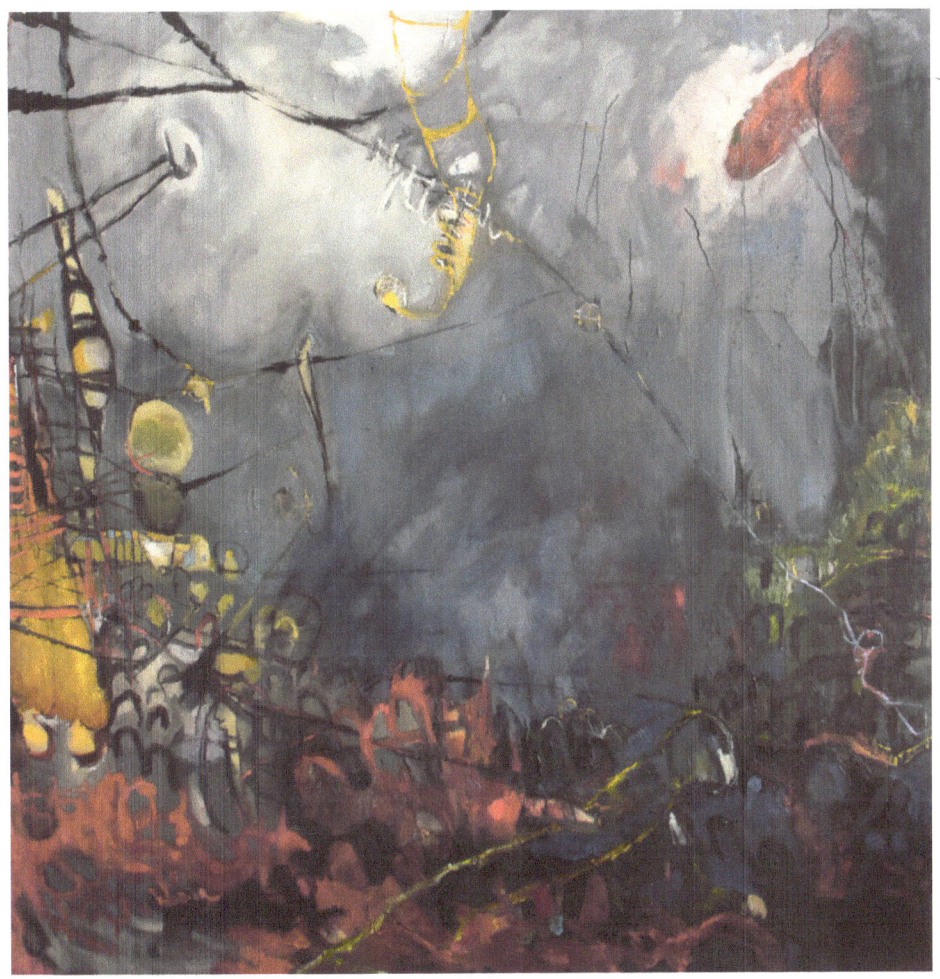

Last Judgement
55" x 55"
Oil paint on linen
2011

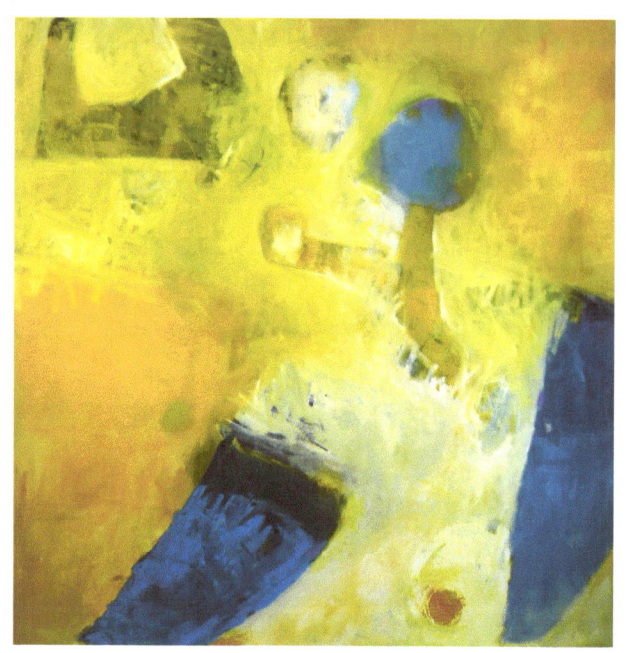

Falling in Love With Icarus
16" x 16"
Mixed media and oil paint on panel
2015

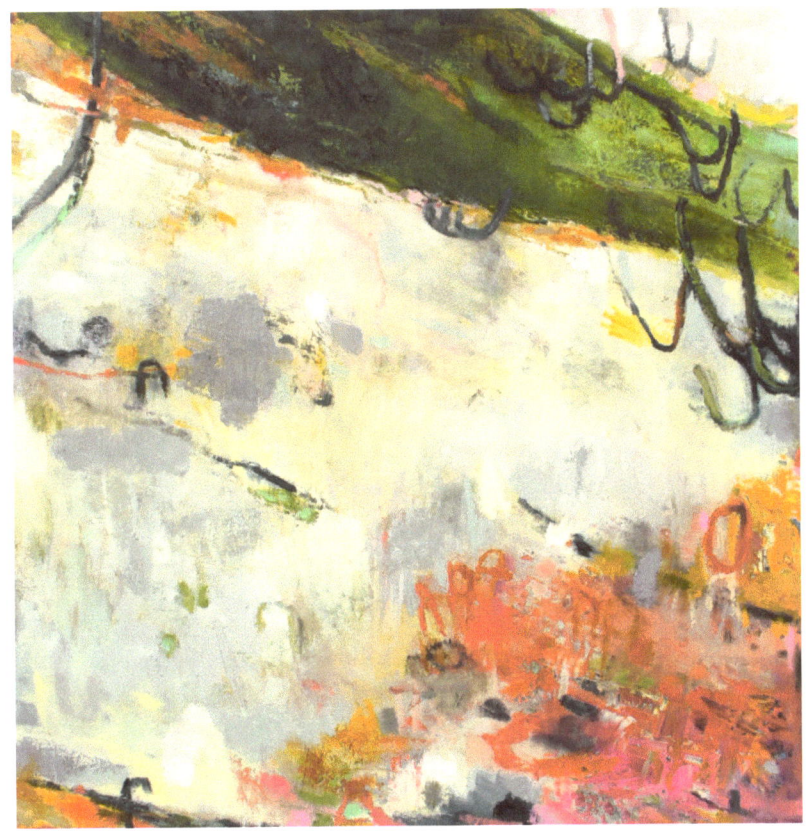

The Crocodile and the Snake Part II
41" x 41"
Oil paint on linen
2014

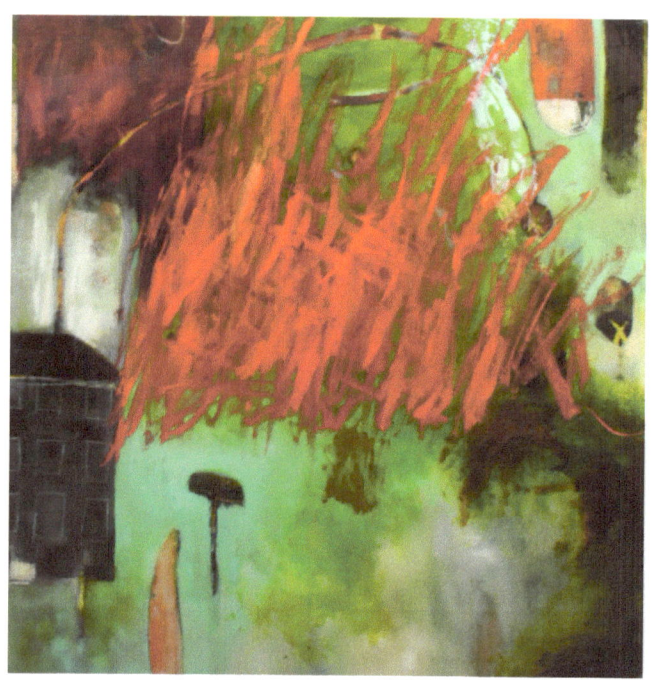

The Triangle Building Fire
16" x 16"
Mixed media and oil paint on panel
2015

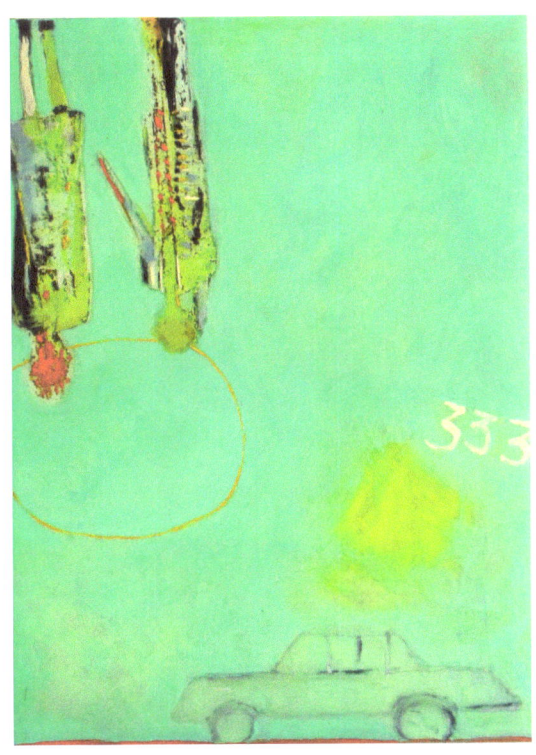

Vertigo
16" x 20"
Mixed media, oil paint and linen on panel
2015

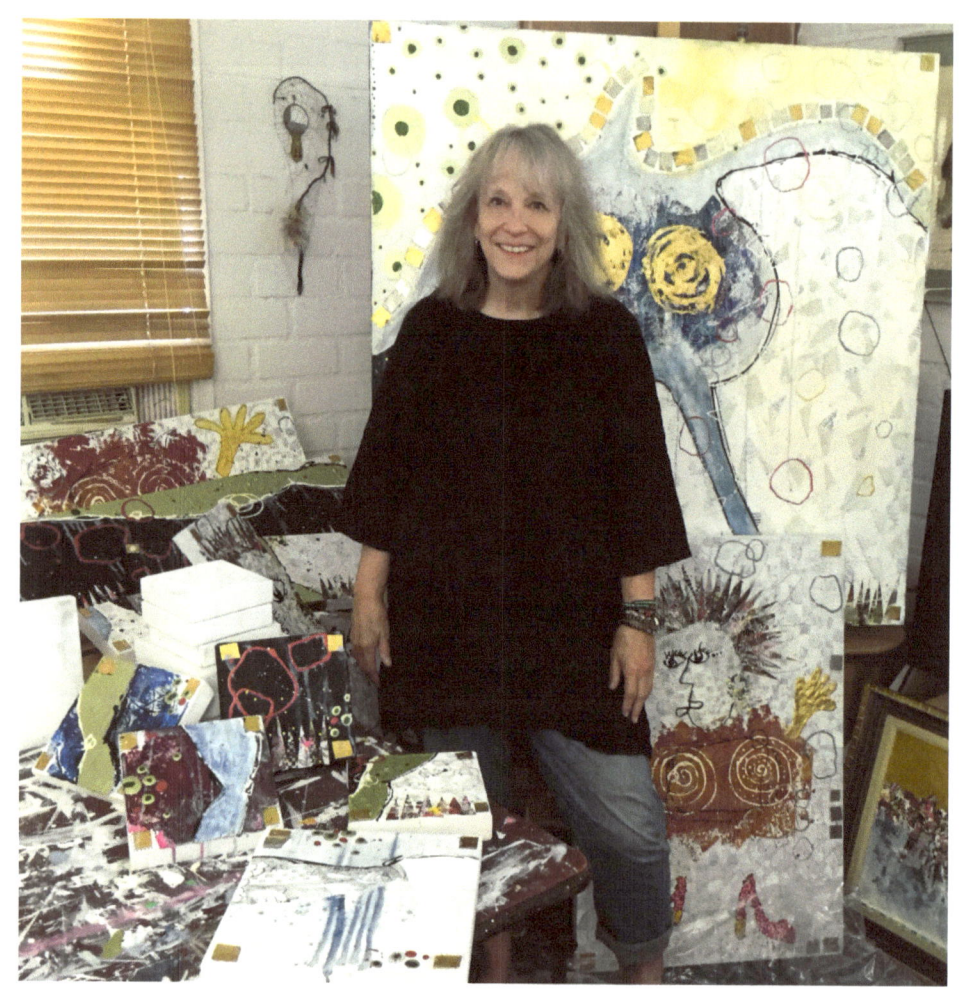

LINE

Karrie Ross

dis·tor·tion

1. the action of distorting or the state of being distorted.

In the definition of the word I took the meaning of 1. the action of distorting or the state of being distorted to share a story with you.

When I was seven years old I ruptured my right eardrum, the thin tissue that separates the ear canal from the middle ear. There was bleeding for what seems like at least a week, I had to sit quietly, which was not easy, and hold a towel up to my ear until it stopped. I didn't experience any loss of hearing, in fact I found I was hearing better, more clearly and vibrations seemed more pronounced. As I've grown older, I noticed that I get motion sickness in cars or planes, and that I walk a little off-kilter — I never thought a thing about it... until I started being more interested in how my life experiences affect my artwork and general view of how I live in the world.

I found I liked the distortion found in the asymmetrical more then symmetrical. This guided me to energy balancing as a healing technique. When we are ill, our body and chemistry is off, distorted. I became obsessed — and the action of this noble obsession makes my art. For if my work is not somewhat distorted I do not see a sense of completion... almost like I'd rather be standing on one foot than two.

The images in L I N E come from recent contour-esk line drawings of people I see when I'm out. You'd never be able to say, "Oh yeah, that looks like so-n-so?" as the line of the drawings are much too distorted, but you might say my work "holds their energy". I also threw in some sexy small pieces... I like ankles, they seem to set off the foot from the calf — like a wrist allows access to the hand and forearm— ankles create the in-between space of angst and attention…etherial balance.

www.karrierossfineart.com

September 2015

LINE

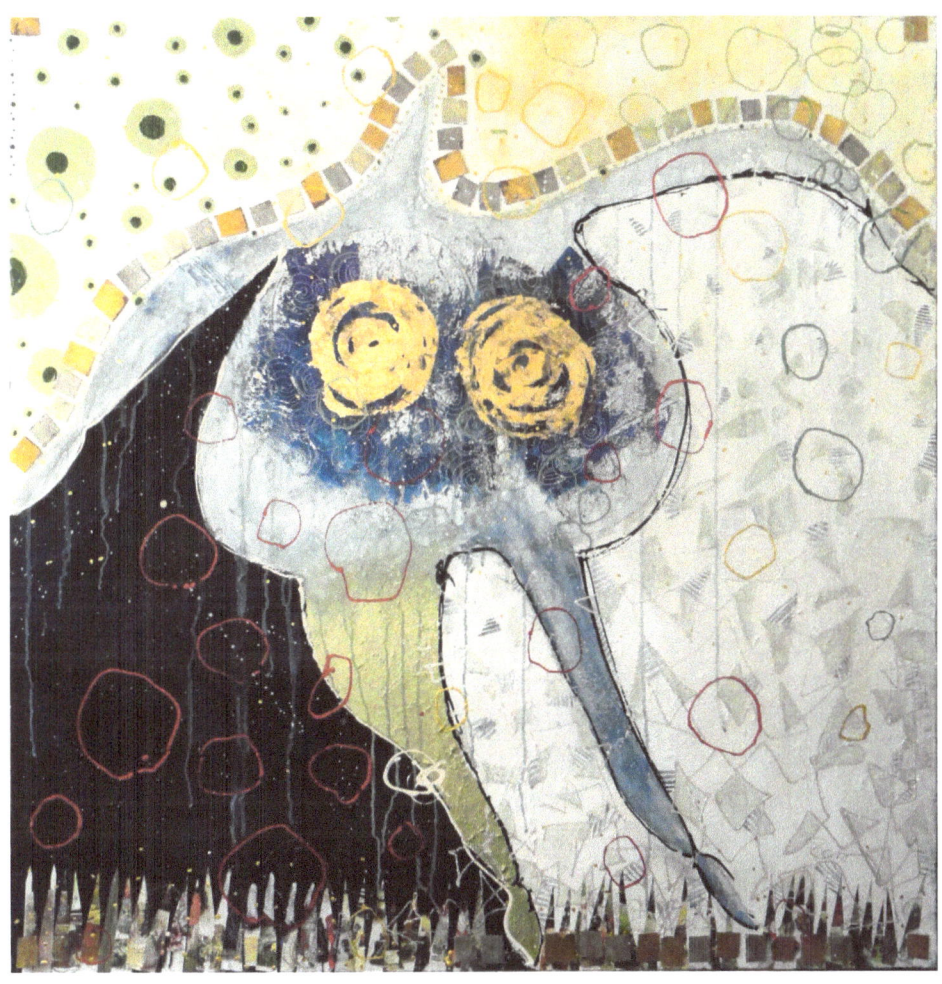

Did You Knotice?
48" x 48"
Oil, acrylic, metal leaf, collage, on canvas
2015

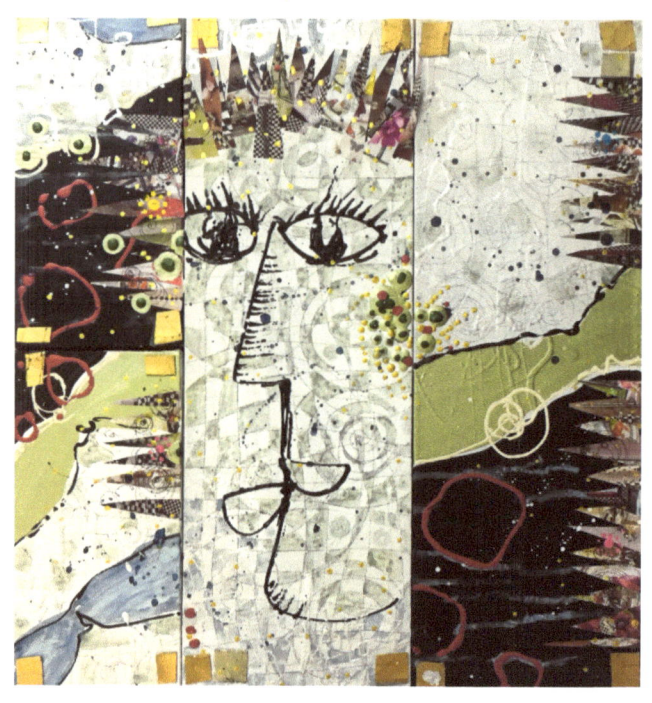

I'm Not Sure What You Mean...?
24x22 four pieces; Two are 8" x 24", Two are 12" x 6"
Oil, acrylic, metal leaf, collage, on canvas
2015

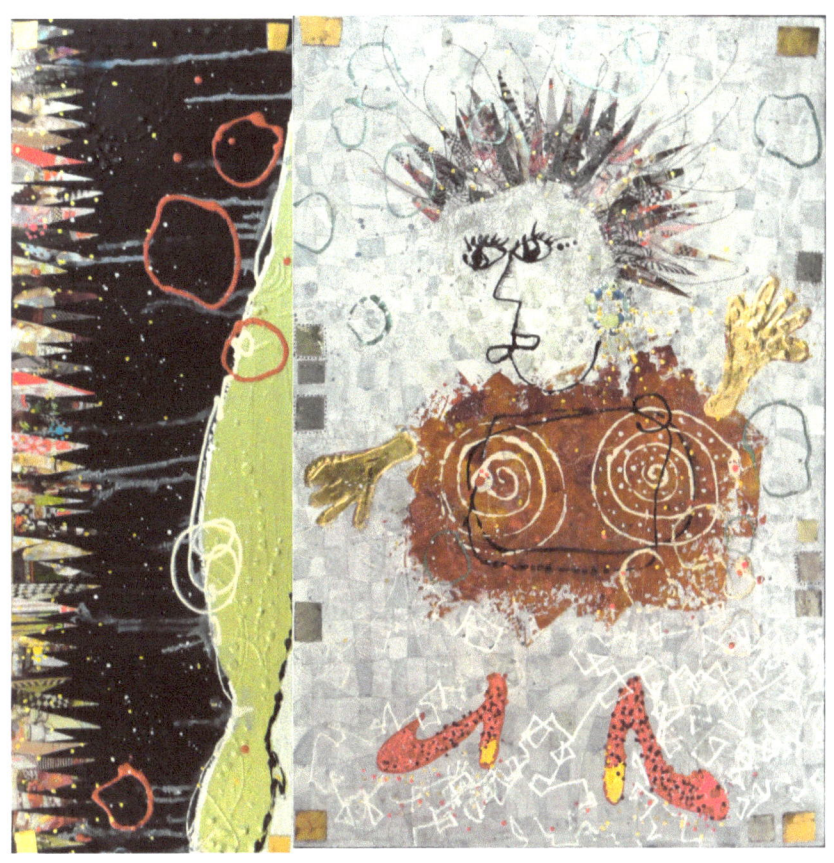

Pink Shoes
36" x 36"; two pieces, left 36" x 12"; right 36" x 24"
Oil, acrylic, metal leaf, collage, on canvas
2015

Moments of Distortion (smalls)
8" x 8"
Oil, acrylic, collage, pencil,
on canvas
2015

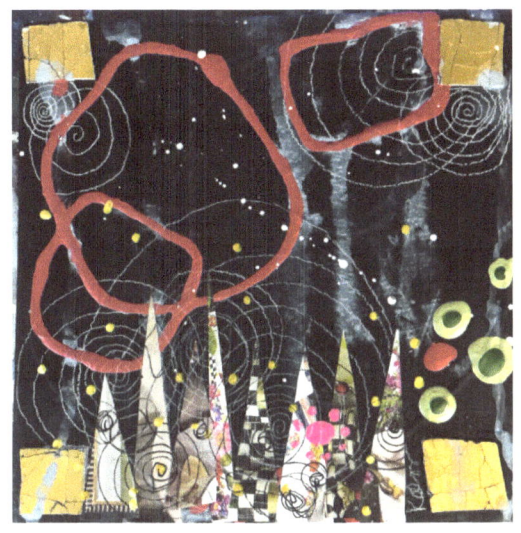
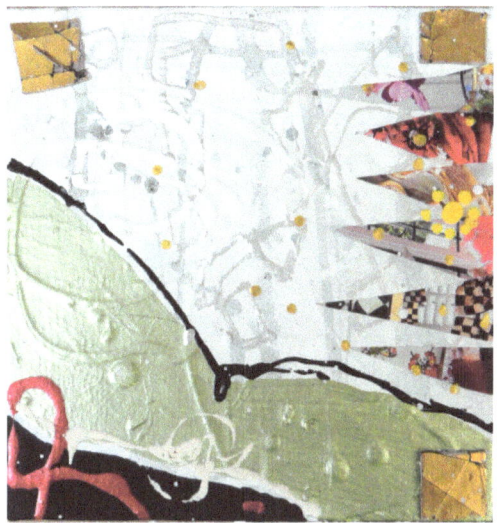
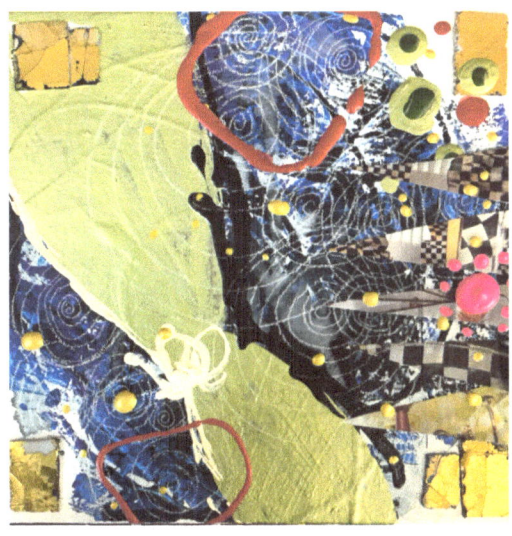
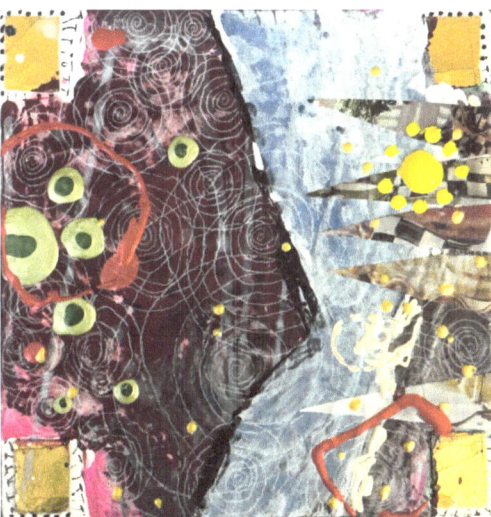

September·2015

Jill Sykes
Beanie Kaman
Emily Elisa Halpern
Karrie Ross

FM Fine Art Gallery
Los Angeles, CA

September 2015.

Line

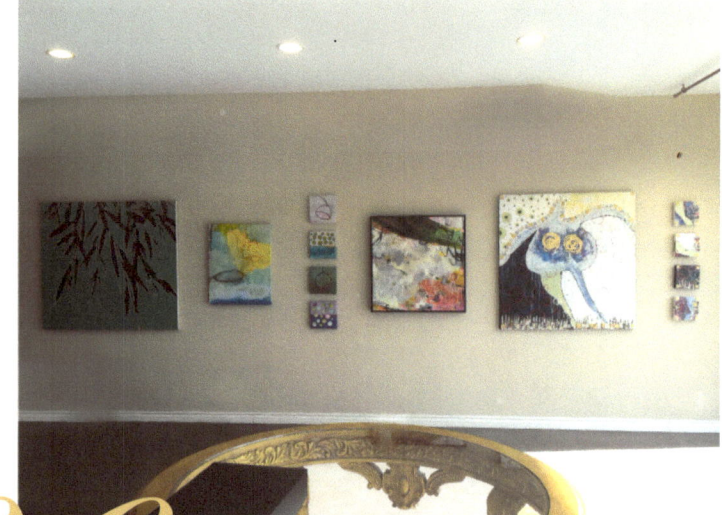

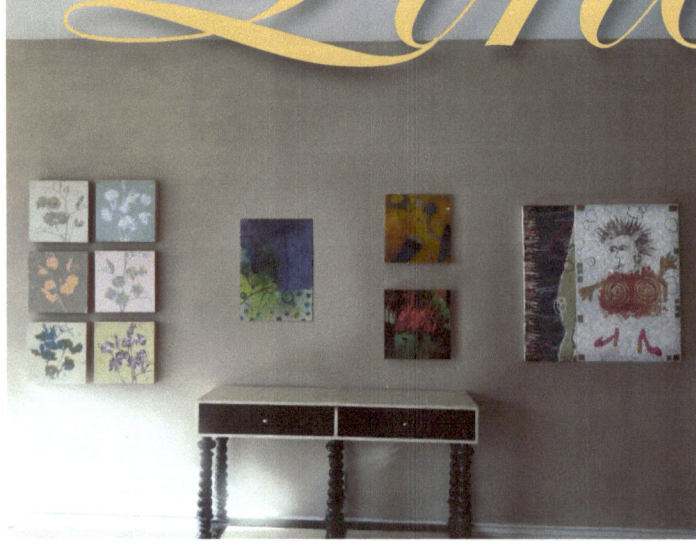

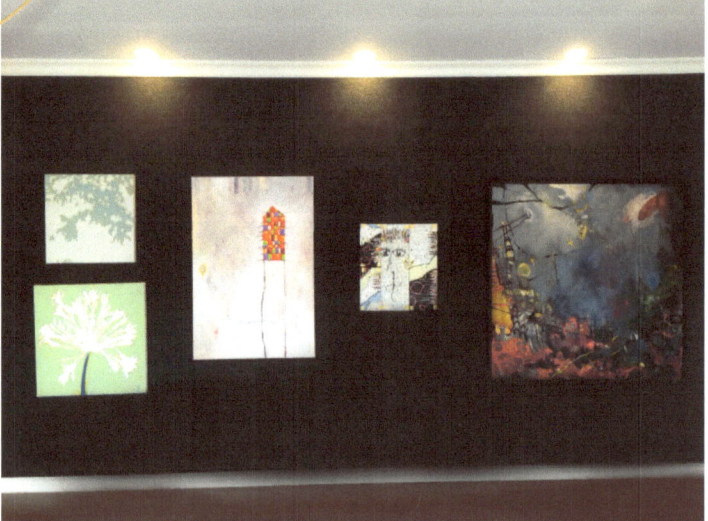

LINE

www.ingramcontent.com/pod-product-compliance
Lightning Source LLC
Chambersburg PA
CBHW050402180526
45159CB00005B/2122